Take Control of Your Future

Answers to Questions about Elder Law & Estate Planning

Douglas E. Koenig, Esq.

Additional copies are available at special quantity discounts for bulk purchases for sales promotions, premiums, fundraising, and educational use.

For more information, please contact:
Law Offices of Douglas E. Koenig, PLLC

Telephone: 919-724-4778
Email: info@dougkoeniglaw.com

The Publisher and Author make no representations or warranties with respect to the accuracy or completeness of the contents of this work and specifically disclaim all warranties, including without limitation warranties of fitness for a particular purpose. No warranty may be created or extended by sales or promotional materials. The advice and strategies contained herein may not be suitable for every situation.

This work is sold with the understanding that the publisher is not engaged in rendering legal, account or other professional services. If professional assistance is required, the services of a competent professional person should be sought. Neither the Publisher nor the Author shall be liable for damages arising here from.

The fact that an organization or website is referred to in this work as a citation and/or potential source of further information does not mean the that Author or Publisher endorses the information the organization or website may provide or recommendations it may make. Further, readers should be aware that the internet websites listed in this work may have changed or disappeared between when this work was written and when it was read.

DEDICATION

To my clients – they become family through our
shared experiences, joy, and pain.

CONTENTS

Acknowledgments i

Introduction 3

Why can I help you? 9

Chapter 1 - Do I Really Need To 'Plan My Estate'? 11

Chapter 2 - What Documents Do I Need To Prepare? 15

Chapter 3 - Don't You Need A Lot Of Money Before Creating An Estate Plan? 19

Chapter 4 - What Will It Cost Me If I Delay Getting My Estate Planning Done... Or Just Don't Do It At All? 21

Chapter 5 – When do People Finally Begin Estate Planning? 25

Chapter 6 - What Do I Need To Know To Plan For My Children's Needs? 29

Chapter 7 - What If I Don't Die But Become Incapacitated? What Would Happen To My Family? 33

Chapter 8 - What Are Trusts, And Why Are They Important In Estate Planning? 35

Chapter 9 – What is a Revocable Trust? 37

Chapter 10 - Once I Establish A Trust, I Can "Take My Hands Off The Wheel," Right? 41

Chapter 11 - Do I Need An Estate Planning Attorney, Specifically, Or Can I Work With A Generalist, Like A Business Lawyer? 43

Chapter 12 – I have more than $5.4 Million. Will Setting Up A Trust Help Me Avoid (Or Minimize) Taxes?............................... 45

Chapter 13 - What Other Tools Can I Use To Craft My Estate Plan? 47

Chapter 14 - Can I Make Changes To My Trust (And Other Documents)? 49

Chapter 15 - What Should I Do About Items That Are Sentimental But Not Valuable? 51

Chapter 16 - How Often Do Tax Laws Change, And What Can I Do About It? 53

Chapter 17 - Why Should I Work With Your Estate Planning Team? 55

About The Author.. 59

Take Action Today!... 63

Acknowledgments

Thanks for the assistance in getting this book ready from Richard James, Jon Alexander, Blaine Olekers, and my wife, Cheryl.

Also, thanks to my clients who have contributed so much to my experiences.

Law Offices of Douglas E. Koenig, PLLC
http://www.dougkoeniglaw.com -- 919-724-4778

Introduction

What drives my passion for Elder Law and for Estate Planning?

One of life's most mysterious and emotional challenges involves confronting our fear of mortality. Humans are the only animals who understand that our lives are finite. Scripture reminds us that "people are destined to die once" (Hebrews 9:27). This knowledge that we won't be around forever on this Earth has profound effects on what we do and why we do it.

Author and philosopher, Ernest Becker, in his book *Denial of Death*, described this challenge in these poignant words:

> "Man cannot endure his own littleness unless he can translate it into meaningfulness on the largest possible level."

Before they come to see me, many clients feel a variety of concerns – many of which they have trouble even expressing clearly – regarding the future and the next generation. For some, the future they fear is related to health and well-being. For others, it is about their legacy.

As their attorney, I have the opportunity to deal with this confusion, uncertainty, and lack of confidence. And, it is important to my clients.

Why? Because fear, confusion, and uncertainty has ramifications for the present!

If you don't feel prepared and protected, it's harder to concentrate on the present – to be spontaneous and free in your personal and business life today.

Helping my clients protect their hard work and assets and wishes is a great honor. To me, the work is not just about creating documents and putting together the estate planning "puzzle" – it's also about providing peace of mind and freedom from worry for people who really need it.

Of course, estate plans *are* puzzles – and fascinating ones at that. Solving them requires many skills: understanding financial planning instruments; knowledge of the law; compassion and a good "bedside manner"; ability to listen and empathize; and creativity.

What I do is fun and interesting and essential to the people who call me their attorney.

In some ways, being an estate planning lawyer is like being a chef. You can choose from many different "spices" and "ingredients" and use an array of "utensils" to prepare nourishing meals, metaphorically speaking. There are hundreds of ways to make a meal, and it is similar in estate planning.

Throughout this book, I'll use examples to make points. These are based on stories and experiences, but don't take anything as "legal advice" … that can only be obtained from a licensed attorney, and only after you sign a written agreement. That said …

Consider Richard, who had an $18 million estate that mostly consisted of real estate parcels divided up into multiple lots. With advanced planning, Richard figured out how to pass these assets to his children and charities that he loved with minimal tax consequences.

But what if Richard had failed to plan? Well, in his case, the exemptions only totaled $5.4 million. That means that *two-thirds* of his estate (around $12 million) could be taxed at a rate as high as *40%*. As a result, $5 million of the estate would go to the government, not to his kids. That wasn't his plan!

Of course, most of us don't have millions to protect. Estate planning isn't important just for people like Richard – folks who have a lot of money and who want to control assets and get shielded from business liability.

Families with young children or elder dependents,

farmers, retirees, entrepreneurs, and everyone in between can benefit from the tools and ideas that I'll be laying out in this book.

Sometimes, planning helps protect family relationships. For instance, take Marissa, a successful entrepreneur and mother of two. Marissa was stunned after her mother's death by the surprising viciousness with which her brother and sister fought over their parent's old home. Despite her best efforts at making peace, she still has not been able to get her brother and sister in the same room – a consequence of her mother and father's lack of planning.

Then there's the case of Helen, an independent farmer who put together an estate plan back when she was in her early 30's. Helen's plan was good at the time, but she took a "set it and forget it" approach to this plan. Forty years later, when she passed away, her children were horrified to discover that the government and creditors took so much of the farm (and its assets) that her legacy was rendered effectively valueless.

Had Helen simply updated her plan regularly as her family and their needs changed, she could have saved the farm and kept it going, perhaps for many generations. Instead, a treasure to her family and the broader community was lost. Her grandchildren, now burdened with student loan debt, could have cleared their credit and started their careers unburdened.

I wrote this book because I'm passionate about helping people gain control over their lives and achieve their good work on Earth. I sincerely hope you enjoy these insights.

If you need more specific and personal help, please skip ahead to the end to learn how to get a free one-hour consultation (normally valued at over $300), so we can strategize together about how to reach your goals in a way that meets your priorities and values.

Elder Law usually involves planning. A lot of it!

Douglas E. Koenig, Esq.

Why can I help you?

First, I know what I'm talking about.

Everything I talk about is a real event or story I gleaned from my clients or my own experiences as a Navy brat or a civilian, as a parent, or as a child. These experiences (no, I didn't use real names or exact situations) help me relate to your stories.

Second, I want to help you.

After 30 years in the business world, I retired from Ford Motor Company in Michigan. But, I didn't stay retired. I opened a law practice aimed at elders and their needs and estate planning. My staff and I want you to age gracefully and with dignity, and to be ready with plans that makes sense for you. We can help you with that.

Third, I'm right there with you.

Thinking about your own retirement? Worried about your aging parents? Concerned about your troubled children?

I am too. I get it. I can help you.

I wrote this book as part of a series about common issues in Elder Law. My hope is that you will gain some clarity about the issues you face, and recognize how you can be ready when life throws you a curve.

Read on, let's get started learning about how you can "Take Control of Your Future"!

Chapter 1 - Do I Really Need To 'Plan My Estate'?

Whether you're an "invincible" healthy young woman in her mid-20s, or a 50-something-year-old entrepreneur on your third big venture, or a person considering how your life will change long after retirement, you probably don't relish the thought of taking time out of your busy life to contemplate what will happen to you when you become unwell and when you die.

This is normal – it's human nature to want to avoid these kinds of conversations.

That said, since you're reading this book, you already understand that you need such plans in place.

But you may not fully appreciate the risks.

Here's a perspective that helps. The late General (and President) Dwight D. Eisenhower once offered the following Yoda-like observation: "plans are useless, but planning is indispensable."

What Eisenhower meant is that the plans you make today – before you go to battle or get sick – will change as circumstances change. It is sometimes said that "Plans do not survive the first battle."

You can never figure out what an enemy will do in a war or how new tax laws will evolve or how the stock market will flow.

However, the act of planning *in and of itself* organizes your life and thoughts and prepares you to meet the surprises of the future with more nimbleness.

Holly had a solid estate plan that reflected her priorities. She got sick with leukemia and had to spend months in the hospital. But she managed her business and finances because she had done the planning work when she was well.

A farm analogy rings true. You sow the field in good weather, so you can reap the harvest and eat in bad weather. Planning when you are well protects you when times change. Preparation helps your family too.

When Rodrigo suddenly died in a car accident, his family (two small children and spouse) might have been in trouble … faced with possible bills, creditors and tax headaches. But because he did plan ahead, and obtained the right insurance and established trusts, Rodrigo shielded his loved ones from creditors, helped his estate bypass estate taxation, and gave his wife money (through the insurance) to raise the family the way they had always planned.

So, yes, you do need to plan your estate.

Your life is fluid, and things change from one minute, day, or year, to the next.

Planning is essential. A key truth I learned over the years is that you can prepare reasonably well for what you see coming ... the harder part is preparing for what you don't anticipate.

You can't build anything, much less a fighter plane or a bridge, without planning and thinking about the moving parts. The same goes for your estate and your future.

Knowing that your plans are solid lets you enjoy life. It's a lot easier (and less scary) to cross a bridge across a chasm when there's a sturdy railing.

Your estate plan can be one part of that railing.

Douglas E. Koenig, Esq.

Chapter 2 - What Documents Do I Need To Prepare?

Once you decide that planning is important, if not indispensable, the next question is how to start the planning. What documents are essential?

Amanda wanted to keep her estate plans simple. As a working mom with two children, she didn't have a lot of time to mull a deep investment strategy or do anything fancy. Plus, she and her husband, Eric, didn't have a lot in savings.

Amanda's aim was to get the "minimum done" before her third child was born and then figure out a more detailed strategy later, when she had breathing room.

This isn't unusual. Many young professional families need something in place that works at a minimum. If she were asking advice, initially, I might tell Amanda to create the following essential documents:

- **Durable power of attorney**. This document is the most important one for most people. It would allow a designated "agent" (usually her husband, Eric, or another trusted person) to make legal decisions for her if she became incapacitated. It needs to be "durable" to be functional after she becomes incapacitated.

- **Advance Directive for Healthcare**. This is also known as the "Living Will" and it provides written guidance for Eric (and for her doctors) about what to do if she reaches the point of death. In particular, the document advises her health care agent(s) about life-sustaining treatments she wants.

- **HIPAA release form**. HIPAA (the Health Information Portability and Accountability Act) is a privacy law designed to protect patients' personal information. HIPAA can be a double-edged sword, since it can prevent people like Eric or Amanda's mother from accessing her medical records and treatment information without having to go through an elaborate process. The HIPAA release bypasses that and allows access when needed.

- **Will or Revocable Trust**. These documents determine how Amanda wants her assets allocated after she dies and provides instructions for her heirs for her family.

For Amanda and Eric, the most important feature of the Will is the naming of possible guardians for her children (in the event that both Amada and Eric are killed in the same car accident).

But, in addition, our discussion revealed other important facts about Amanda that can't be discovered when you ask an attorney only for "estate planning documents".

As it turned out, Amanda wasn't just "working"; she was a very successful internet blogger and marketer. And, she and Eric had several pets, with specific care issues. I advised Amanda that she might also want to include a section in each of these documents detailing what she wants done with her computer files and popular blog, using so-called "digital assets" instructions. In addition, we added sections to her will to cover special items she owned, and a pet trust.

An important note: Please recognize that a will is just a statement of intention to the court. It suggests where you want your assets to go and who should be the executor and who should be named as guardians for the children. A judge must say the will is valid before it goes into effect, legally speaking. But, never let that stop you from planning … if you don't plan, you never know who will be making decisions!

Back to Amanda … if Amanda and Eric had set up a Trust, other rules may apply to the assets in the Trust. There are many types of trusts for many different purposes. For example, had one of their children been a special needs child, we would have developed a "special needs trust" for the family.

In most cases, for a young family like Amanda and Eric's, a trust is not a requirement. But, without planning, and in-depth discussions, we would not know for sure.

With that basic preparation done, Amanda (and Eric) can feel more secure, although she'd likely benefit from a more detailed strategy and a regular reassessment of her financial needs and her family priorities, and a continued discussion about trusts.

As the family grows and changes, its needs will change, and so should the documents and the plan.

Do you have the five essential estate planning documents? If not, **now** is the time to call an estate planning attorney and get started.

Do you have parents, or children, with special needs? Or an unusual possession? Be sure to tell your attorney so the right plans can be made.

Chapter 3 - Don't You Need A Lot Of Money Before Creating An Estate Plan?

Absolutely not. Estate planning helps people of every income bracket. And that is because estate planning is about more than money.

For instance, take Charles. His sister, Nancy, was diagnosed on the autism spectrum. Their father (the last surviving parent) died without putting together an estate plan. Nancy had lived at home with her father; she had a part-time volunteer job and limited connections in the neighborhood because of her disability. And, she was receiving SSI (supplemental security income) because she was unable to work.

Their father had run a small retail business that wasn't worth much when he died, so there wasn't much in the bank accounts to pass to the children. But he bought his home back in the 1960s, and the property was now worth much more than when it was purchased.

Charles's plan was to sell the home and split the proceeds with his sister Nancy. But there was a big problem. If Nancy inherited these assets, she would become ineligible to collect Supplemental Security Income (SSI) benefits. She needed that money to pay for day-to-day things like clothes, groceries, medical needs, and so on.

Had their father planned better, he could have directed that Nancy's share of his assets be placed into a "Supplemental Needs Trust" (SNT) for Nancy. Then, funds from the home sale and what was left of his bank accounts would protect Nancy while keeping her eligible for SSI benefits.

Fortunately, Charles consulted an attorney and found that he could fix the problem by asking a court to establish a specific form of special needs trust. Charles was named to serve as a trustee. Nancy would continue to receive SSI, and the trust could purchase important things for her.

Sadly, the process took time and expense, yet both would have been unnecessary had Nancy's father planned in advance.

In another case, a young family with two small children did not plan for guardians for their children. When the parents were killed in a car accident while returning from dinner one night, the court had no recommendations for guardianships. The remaining family fought for years over who should be able to raise the children, which caused costs, trouble, and frustration for all involved.

The moral here is this: planning is a "must-do" project, not a "would like to do if I have the time one day" project. Call an estate attorney today!

Chapter 4 - What Will It Cost Me If I Delay Getting My Estate Planning Done... Or Just Don't Do It At All?

The costs in terms of money, time, and peace of mind for you and your family could be huge.

But shockingly, 55% of Americans die without estate plans. In North Carolina, that total may be as high as 65%. Why is that?

To answer that, let's turn to bestselling author, Stephen Covey ("The 7 Habits of Highly Effective People"), who built a quadrant model to discuss how people prioritize things. Per Covey:

- **Quadrant 1 activities are urgent and important**, such as paying your taxes when they are due. We get them done, but we don't plan for that very well. And, if you are a procrastinator, you might find yourself waiting until the last minute for every deadline.

- **Quadrant 3 activities are urgent but not important,** such as watching a football game on Sunday night. We tend to respond to the "latest and loudest," so most people do a lot of Quadrant 1 and 3 things.

- **Quadrant 4 concerns activities that are neither important, nor urgent**, such as playing online games or checking email or other social media sites while at work. Most of us spend far more time in Quadrant 4 than we'd like to admit!

- **Quadrant 2 is unique. It concerns *important* activities that are not urgent.** Playing with your children instead of working another hour might fit this category. And, Estate planning falls squarely in Quadrant 2. Because facing the idea of dying gets pushed out of our minds, we don't see the urgency of estate planning, even though we might understand the importance.

The more time and energy we devote to the Quadrant 2 activities, the richer and better our lives, and legacy, become. But living and working in Quadrant 2 requires personal focus as well as a deep appreciation of what really matters in life.

Keep that in mind as we go through the following example.

Consider the case of Rosaline. After her sister died, she hired a probate and estate planning lawyer to handle the estate. Rosaline was 64, and her sister, Carolyn, was 75 when she died.

Carolyn had done a minimal amount of planning, and she had a will, but not a trust, forcing the estate to be probated. The probate process took time and money, and Rosaline had to spend funds from the estate that her nephews and their families could have had. In addition, the process took several years because Carolyn had property in other states.

Carolyn's sense of urgency was too low for estate planning, so her estate was diminished unnecessarily.

It didn't stop there. Although Rosaline saw the cumbersome probate process for what it was, she refused to get her own estate plan in order. In fact, she spent *11 years* avoiding the work. Why? Because she was estranged from her son, who had left the house when he was a teenager and who had avoided contact with his mother ever since.

As Rosaline grew older, she tried to find and reconnect with her son – who, at this point, was in his 50s. But he still refused to see her. And since he was her only child, Rosaline abandoned the idea of planning. Without the apparent need to plan for her son's benefit, she lost any send of urgency to plan.

When she finally passed away, her younger brother, Albert, contacted the same probate and estate planning attorney who worked on Carolyn's estate long ago.

They both assumed Rosaline's estate would be modest, but it turned out to be worth over $1.4 million. Unfortunately, probate costs, legal fees and taxes stripped Rosaline's estate of much of its value – money that could have been earmarked for a good cause, like a charity, scholarships, or even her younger brother's children's education.

Estate planning is not just about *your* comfort level and needs. It's also about your *legacy* – about your family, your friends, the causes you believe in, the good work you do on earth.

When you fail to plan, you don't just hurt yourself or your estate … you also, in effect, turn your back on those who need your help.

What are you putting off? Do you have a "plan" to get estate planning done … someday?

If you are not sure that your current plans will do what you want and need for your family, **now** is the time to call an estate planning attorney!

Chapter 5 – When do People Finally Begin Estate Planning?

Why do people finally start to plan? What causes them to "get with the program"?

Unfortunately, the event that makes people think is usually tragic.

Lance had an epiphany. His best friend from college, Loren, suffered a massive coronary while hiking in the Sierra Nevada's and dropped dead on the trail. It was a chilling reminder to Lance that he wouldn't live forever.

Dennis, meanwhile, was 37 with two children. A blood test revealed bad news: elevated triglycerides, low HDL cholesterol, and pre-diabetes. Not a terminal diagnosis, but cause for alarm.

Reminders of mortality can often motivate even the most reluctant to do their estate planning.

Sometimes, it is simply a sudden realization of change that strikes a person, or a family. They see events, or their situation, from a new perspective and planning makes more sense.

Julianne and Roger were parents totally in love with their 6-year-old and 2-year-old kids. But, we all know as parents that sometimes we need time to reconnect as a couple. It is healthy to step back and and breathe free from time to time, especially as parents of very young children.

So they left their children with Julianne's parents and got plane tickets to Rome. The plan was simple... drink fine wine, eat amazing food, sleep a lot, and live uninterruptedly for a weekend for the first time in years.

To their surprise, though, Julianne and Roger's conversation on the first night turned to the kids. Being 5,000 miles away from them for the first time ever, they suddenly realized what was at stake. What if something happened to the two of them? Who would take care of the kids?

Julianne's parents were older, Roger's were no longer alive, and Roger's younger brother (the only sibling either had) was less than frugal financially and who was in bad debt. This weekend dinner in Rome became the existential wakeup call that they needed to get their estate planning done.

Finally, it isn't always mortality, or tragedy that makes us think. Sometimes, it is success.

Success was the trigger that inspired Tamara. She hadn't really considered what to do with her money because, frankly, she didn't have much, until her online business took off.

She suddenly found herself with 30,000 newsletter subscribers and a monthly income of $70,000. This influx of cash excited but also overwhelmed her, and reminded her to be responsible.

She still remembered what happened when her grandfather who didn't plan was diagnosed with dementia. Without a plan, health care took its toll, and consumed her grandfather's assets.

Tamara decided to make plans to protect her assets, as well as prepare her family for uncertain times. Even with success, the future is not guaranteed.

How will your family fare? Do you have plans? Have you had an event that caused you to pick up this book? If so, **now** is the time to call an attorney and discuss planning.

In our practice, we usually encourage a team approach, including financial planning, estate planning, and spiritual planning. No, we are not the only ones who can help you, but an estate planning attorney is an important place to start.

Douglas E. Koenig, Esq.

Chapter 6 - What Do I Need To Know To Plan For My Children's Needs?

So far, we've mentioned several different times that planning for children is one important part of estate planning. You might be asking, what is involved? What do I need to know? Our clients often start with a few basic questions.

Maria avoided planning her estate until she got pregnant with her second child, and she only really started planning because she read an internet article that scared her into action. So she buckled down and answered the following five questions.

1. ***Who would be good parents for my children?***

   Not every person would be a good fit. The decision is important, and should reflect your confidence as to their ability to care for any children, to care for *your* children, and to be responsible as "parents".

   Maria has several siblings to choose from, but not all people choose siblings as potential guardians. Sometimes your best friends with children the ages of your children might be a good and logical choice.

In Maria's case, she and her husband decided that her brother would be the best fit, if necessary, because of his love for their children and his close ties to the extended family in Mexico.

2. How could they afford to care for my children, if forced to do so suddenly?

Your choice for guardians implies a cost the potential "parents" might not have planned for, especially if they don't have children of their own now. The role of guardian of your children can be supported by assets from your estate, or by life insurance. You can plan with trusts or make a trust beneficiary of insurance.

Maria and her husband decided to purchase term life insurance that could be used to support the children if necessary, and to fund their college educations.

3. If someone else needed to raise my kids, what parenting philosophy would I want him or her to follow?

Your proposed guardians for the children will not believe exactly what you do. It might be close, but it won't be what you would have taught them yourself. You can take steps to help guide their experiences.

Maria wanted her brother, David, to raise the kids if anything happened to both Maria and her husband. But David had odd habits and a liberal worldview that she didn't want to pass onto her children.

So she wrote a letter to David that suggested that he should teach the kids compassion, moderation, and respect for others. She suggested several books that guided her own beliefs in her youth, and she requested that David bring the kids to various museums and cultural events that she felt would expand her children's views.

She also wanted the kids to learn Spanish and make regular trips to see her parents, their *abuela* and *abuelo,* in Mexico on a regular basis.

4. *What values, religious and otherwise, do I want to pass along?*

Religion is a deeply personal subject, and most parents do want to pass along the basis for their spiritual beliefs. That isn't as easy for the guardian. So, to help explain it, some people share their beliefs in a letter to the children and the guardian.

A self-described Catholic, Maria thought it was important to teach her children her spiritual heritage and the importance of community giving. She wanted David to take her children to church for Sunday school or catechism and for them to have the chance to decide for themselves what their beliefs should be. Her letter to her kids was a story of her own faith journey.

5. What do we want our children to know about our life story?

All families have a history that children learn from family events and gatherings. But, if your children suddenly end up in another family, how would they learn? Some families also share medical issues that are family related in case the children ever need to know.

Maria and her husband wrote out a short family history and a family tree. They left this in their estate planning binder so that their families would find it and be able to share it with the guardians and others. They included the stories of their families, and how they met, but also described how important it was for them to have children and how much they loved them.

Chapter 7 - What If I Don't Die But Become Incapacitated? What Would Happen To My Family?

Incapacity Planning is the subject of entire books. It is the process of determining who will care for you and how they should do so.

If you are incapacitated for any period of time, someone will need to make medical and financial decisions for you. This person is called the "agent". The agent has only the powers you give them, unless they are granted by a court in a "guardianship" proceeding. But, you have some control, and it is wise to use it to make the plans you want.

The tools used by estate planning attorneys are called "Powers of Attorney" (POA), and they can be designed to grant medical or financial powers. Medical powers include such things as deciding your course of medical care, or deciding when you should be removed from life support, and more. Financial powers include banking, investments, selling real estate, and so on. You really need both sets to be fully protected.

What happens if you don't plan using these documents? Sometimes it does not turn out well for the person involved at all.

Michael was a self-described "born slacker" who always waited until the last minute to do everything – to turn in assignments in school, to file his taxes, to get his estate planning done. In addition, he took the short-cuts for everything, so he did the bare minimum ... it was "enough", so he thought.

Unfortunately, this "slacker" tendency meant that he took a short cut in estate planning. And, his poor discipline caused an accident while sky-diving. The bad accident left him comatose and unable to care for his children. When his estate planning attorney went through his documents, she found that he only had a will, written before he had children or an ex-wife. He did not have a trust or any organized documents to determine how to pay his bills or care for his family. He had no disability insurance, and no records of where his assets were. Without a financial POA, no one was in charge of his investments.

Fortunately, his estate attorney managed to triage the situation, but her legal fees (and other costs to the estate), his medical bills, and court costs for guardianship ate away at Michael's savings, leaving his young children with little to rebuild their lives.

Do you have proper financial and health care Powers of Attorney? If not, **now** is the time to call an estate attorney… before it is too late.

Chapter 8 - What Are Trusts, And Why Are They Important In Estate Planning?

A Trust is an agreement, or a "contract", between its maker (sometimes called the grantor) and a trustee, who manages that property for the benefit of another person or entity.

Under that agreement, the trust maker transfers assets to the trustee and instructs the trustee as to how to manage assets held in the trust. The instructions specify how the assets are used during the maker's lifetime, as well as how the assets are to be distributed following the maker's death. Trusts can be simple, or very complicated.

Unlike Wills that operate only after your death, Trusts can provide a way to manage your assets while you are living … during periods of disability or incapacity. Trusts also avoid probate and the costs and time associated with probate.

An example with names might help. James has two children, Martha and Olive. He wants his estate to go to the kids, but they are too young to receive any of his money if he dies. James, needs a trusted friend to help manage the money, in case James dies earlier than he plans. James decides to set up a trust for his children… who has what role?

James is known as the "Grantor", also sometimes called the trust "Maker". Martha and Olive, the people who benefit from the trust, are known as the "Beneficiaries." James names his CPA as the "Trustee".

James sadly passes on at the early age of 55, and now those assets need to be transferred to his children. But someone must pay taxes on the assets, handle creditors who might want some of the property, and deal with other logistical and liability issues.

The trustee, James' CPA, is the person who deals with all that administrative management.

Why do people use this type of instrument?

It makes the process of distributing assets a lot simpler. If you only use a will, the law will mandate that your assets get passed through probate, so they can be tracked and organized.

Do you have property in other states? Do you worry about your young children? Do you simply want to avoid probate?

If any of those are your concerns, talk to an estate planning or elder law attorney today!

Chapter 9 – What is a Revocable Trust?

In articles about You will see the terms "Revocable" trusts and "Irrevocable" trusts. They are very different and are used for specific reasons. So, you might be asking, what is a "Revocable Trust"?

The term "revocable" refers to the fact that the maker has the power to change or do away with the trust. The maker also has the power to add or remove assets from the trust and control and direct all payments from the trust. If the maker is also the trustee, he or she can make all decisions concerning the assets in the trust. The assets titled in a revocable trust will avoid probate at the maker's death.

Trusts can be created while a person is still living, or as part of a Last Will and Testament ("Will").

A trust created at your death, using the Will, is called a "testamentary" trust (and it is usually not revocable). A "living trust" is just a type of revocable trust that is created while the maker is alive, as opposed to a trust that is made using a Last Will and Testament.

Some trusts cannot be changed… these are called "irrevocable". So, what is an "Irrevocable Trust"?

An irrevocable trust is simply a type of trust that **cannot** be changed after the agreement has been signed. It may also be a revocable trust that becomes irrevocable after the Trust maker dies (it probably isn't a surprise that this can happen because the trust maker is no longer alive to direct the trust options).

Many of our clients are looking for a way to save on federal estate taxes. Since the recent rules for federal estate taxes changed, the rules expanded the limit for estate taxes. Consequently, trusts used to minimize federal taxes are less common. In fact, few families have assets in excess of $5.4 million, or twice that for a married couple. But that isn't the only tax a trust can help avoid.

Both wills and trusts can help avoid estate taxes, but must include specific provisions to do so.

Living Trusts are tax neutral because the Trust maker still owns the assets, and so there is no particular tax applied to assets in the trust.

Irrevocable trusts can accomplish several estate planning goals, including asset protection and estate tax reduction. Other trusts can be used to maintain the "step-up" in basis use to reduce capital gains taxes on appreciated assets (such as your home, which may have gained in value since you bought it).

If you require tax planning, you should make sure that an experienced estate planning attorney handles your planning, whether you choose to do so by Will or Trust.

Some types of trusts are designed primarily for elders to protect their access to public benefits.

Elder clients often tend to use a special type of Irrevocable Trust for Medicaid and VA planning. This trust permanently places a grantors asset out of his or her reach for purposes of legally qualifying for some federal benefits. This is an especially complex area of the law, with constantly changing rules. If you think you need Medicaid planning, or you are a veteran, see an estate planning attorney versed in these specific issues.

Finally, some families have to consider the needs of disabled family members. A special needs trust (SNT), is also known as a supplemental needs trust. It is a special type of irrevocable trust used when a disabled person needs assets protected for their use above and beyond benefits provided by federal or state benefit plans.

When we work with clients, we usually ask a number of questions designed to determine if a trust makes sense for them. Working with trusts is not a cookie-cutter process.

Do you fit any of these complex categories? Are you a veteran? Do you have children or parents with special needs? Are your family members receiving public benefits, including SSI, SSDI, VA pension or disability, or Medicaid?

If so, you might need a specialty trust of one type or another. Don't make this decision alone ... call an elder law or estate planning attorney today.

Chapter 10 - Once I Establish A Trust, I Can "Take My Hands Off The Wheel," Right?

If you have taken the time to set up a plan, congratulations! If you haven't - do it soon. And once you do, all is good, right?

Not necessarily.

Many estate plans utilize a tool known as a "trust". A trust is a contract between the person giving funds to the trust (the "grantor") and the person managing the trust and the funds (the "trustee"). But, note, a trust must have assets, or funds, or investments in it for the trustee to manage.

If you forget to place assets in trust, those assets will end up in probate, creating headaches for your beneficiaries. Plus, tax laws and relevant rules and regulations change over time, creating both opportunities and obstacles.

Think about establishing a trust (or any estate planning solution) as like going to the doctor or buying a car. It's not a 'set it and forget it' proposition. Some maintenance is required to ensure that the documents and the plan works for you.

We encourage our clients to review their estate plans

from time to time. Advance care planning is a process, not a onetime event, and your wishes may change as circumstances change. You should review your choices whenever any of the "Decision D's" occur:

- **Doctor**: Review your wishes every time you have a physical exam

- **Decade**: Your 60th, 70th birthday, and so on

- **Death**: of a loved one (or Birth)

- **Divorce**: yourself or a close family member

- **Diagnosis**: Dementia or other progressive illness

- **Decline**: when you (or others) notice a decline in your health

- **Desires change**: As in the case of family estrangements

- **Dedications**: such as gifts or charities

- **Distribution**: such as for an annuity that pays out on a family Inheritance

Exactly when to do a review is a matter of personal taste. But, you should think about all these "decision-Ds" and if you have experienced any of these events, it might be a good time to call your estate planning attorney.

Chapter 11 - Do I Need An Estate Planning Attorney, Specifically, Or Can I Work With A Generalist, Like A Business Lawyer?

Most of our clients have a friend, or know someone who is an attorney. Some have family members who know a lot about the law. And, you will hear from the "public" that any attorney can draft a "will". Sure. But, we have spent a lot of time talking about "planning" and not about documents.

"Drafting a will" is simply writing a document. You can even get documents that look good from the Internet. But, is that what you need?

Consider this cautionary tale. Susan was a lawyer who had a business law background. She took care of her father's estate before he died, which wasn't complex. She thought she had crossed all the "t's" and dotted all the "i's". Her law background made her confident that she had done what was necessary. However, when her father passed away, she discovered $150,000 in property in another state that she hadn't properly moved into the trust.

This asset had to be funneled through the probate process in both the state in which her father died and in the state the property was actually in. This led to thousands of dollars in unnecessary fees, and a very long supplemental probate process.

The moral of Susan's story is that, sometimes in life, you need to acknowledge your limitations and trust someone who has more experience. Susan's law experience was excellent, but did not prepare her to ask all the right questions. Law is a very specific field, and words are precise. Each branch of the Law really does have its own vocabulary.

Look at this in another way. You go to your dentist for regular checkups, but you choose an oral surgeon for delicate facial reconstructive surgery. Similarly, when you're planning your financial future, you should work with a financial planner, and not the bank teller. And, you don't take your car for collision repairs to the oil-change place.

Are you ready for estate planning? Have you decided that this important area of your life needs a checkup? If you are going to work on estate planning, opt to work with someone who handles estate planning day-in, day-out and who works with clients with a similar financial background. If you are an elder, or are helping to plan for life transitions with an elder, go to an elder law attorney.

Today is a good day to call!

Chapter 12 – I have more than $5.4 Million. Will Setting Up A Trust Help Me Avoid (Or Minimize) Taxes?

It can, under certain circumstances.

Remember Richard from early in our book, who had the $18 million in real estate?

As we discussed earlier, Richard had just $5.4 million in federal exemptions, which meant that more than $12 million of his holdings would be taxed at a higher rate.

One solution for him might be to take $5.4 million and distribute it to his children immediately. He could do this with a trust fund. He can then define a testamentary Marital Trust for his wife with another $5.4 million. That trust would effectively be for his wife who, while living, would be the beneficiary of any income and all the principal produced by the real estate held in trust.

So after he dies, Richard's wife has protection, and when she dies, the remainder of the money will then pass through to his children.

This is an over simplification to demonstrate a point. But Richard's whole goal here is to reduce his taxable estate and thus cut his tax down significantly.

No trust (or any other estate planning instrument) can work magic. There are limitations to what can be accomplished in terms of tax savings and other benefits.

But wielded skillfully, these tools can be quite powerful, provided that you plan enough in advance and understand the technical details of the instruments.

Chapter 13 - What Other Tools Can I Use To Craft My Estate Plan?

The catalogue is long and complex and includes lots of possibilities, including: family limited partnerships, LLCs, Medicaid asset protection trusts, bridge trusts, gun trusts, charitable gift annuities, third party asset protection trusts, special needs trusts, the list goes on! At one point, we counted over 100 different types of estate planning documents in use in our practice. The good news is that you only need a few. But, you need the right ones, for the right reasons, at the right time. And, that takes "estate planning"!

The challenge, of course, is knowing when and how to use these tools and under what circumstances. Just like you can walk into a restaurant supply shop and buy all manner of ingredients and utensils, it's hard to prep a 12-course restaurant quality dinner if you've never been in the kitchen before. Internet research and determination won't cut it. You really need to know what you're doing and why.

Douglas E. Koenig, Esq.

Chapter 14 - Can I Make Changes To My Trust (And Other Documents)?

Earlier, we mentioned that you have to consider changes in your life and how they might change your estate plans. So, yes, you can (*and should*) change plans when your needs change.

Thus, the answer to the question depends on what kind of trust (or instrument) you've established and what timeframes and other rules and restrictions govern the situation.

In general, the more sophisticated and complex the planning, the more moving parts there will be, and the more challenging it will be to shift things around without getting into trouble.

At the same time, some decisions cannot be changed for various reasons. If, for example, you set up an irrevocable trust for Medicaid planning, you cannot later change your mind to get back to the assets. And, if you are thinking of changing a document that requires your capacity to sign it, you have to have capacity. If your lawyer, or a doctor, certify that you have lost capacity, you won't be able to make changes.

The nature and size of the assets that you lay away in the trust (or other vehicle) can also be important.

For instances, Teddy purchased a house 30 years ago for $400,000. Today, thanks to appreciation (and location), it's worth $6 million. He and his wife want to leave the house evenly to all three children, so each will get $2 million in value. To shield his children from so-called "creditors and predators," Teddy could establish a trust that allows each child access to $2 million. This act would prevent "outlaw in laws" and creditors and others from touching the money. Teddy might alternatively create incentive trusts, like educational trusts, which would reward his children for doing things like getting their college or advanced degrees or would distribute funds over time to curtail the chance of reckless spending.

If you have documents in an estate plan that need to be changed, consult an estate planning attorney before making changes. It is better to ask a few simple questions than to break the plans you worked so hard to establish.

Chapter 15 - What Should I Do About Items That Are Sentimental But Not Valuable?

Disputes over seemingly low value assets that are nevertheless sentimentally important can wreck families.

Famously, in 2015, Robin Williams's family got involved in a bitter dispute over what to do with the late actor's Hollywood memorabilia. Should it go to his wife or his children? The public legal battle demonstrated how debates over sentimental items motivate people and fuel passions.

In some cases, sentimental items might be unavailable to the family for legal reasons. Your advance planning can help avoid this.

Margaret planed very well. She placed her assets in a revocable trust many years ago, and had well defined rules for management and eventual distribution. However, even though all her assets were in the trust, no one had ever thought about her keepsakes all over the house. When Margaret died, her final expenses and the administrative fees were due, but there was literally no money in her estate to pay the bills. The executor had no choice but to auction off the keepsakes and pictures from an entire lifetime to pay the bills. The family did not get to keep any of her keepsakes.

She could have easily avoided this by placing her personal possessions into the trust too.

What can you learn from this? Be as specific as possible with respect to your assets. Itemize exactly what you want done with this type of property and how you want to do it. Leave little room for interpretation or error.

This rule of thumb also goes for things like pet planning. If you own a beloved dog or cat, create exact provisions for who will care for the animal and how. The fewer details you leave to chance and negotiation – particularly when it comes to sentimental assets – the better.

Chapter 16 - How Often Do Tax Laws Change, And What Can I Do About It?

To make trade flow smoothly, legislatures generally try to avoid altering tax laws too radically and too often. Otherwise, consumers could not plan, and businesses would adopt ultra conservative postures, causing the economy to stagnate.

However, just because tax law evolves slowly and conservatively doesn't mean it's frozen solid.

Congress can change federal tax laws at any time, and local and state tax laws also shift. These modifications can have big implications for your plans. As we've discussed, the best way to protect yourself and ensure your plan reflects your priorities and values is to reevaluate it at regular intervals – for instance, every year or any time a major life event (e.g. your daughter gets married) occurs.

Douglas E. Koenig, Esq.

Chapter 17 - Why Should I Work With Your Estate Planning Team?

If you're a do-it-yourself-er, you might be tempted to "have a go" at creating your own estate plan using tools available online. But the estate planning process is not simple. You have to understand many technical rules and address them skillfully.

Remember Susan, the business attorney who did her mother's planning and accidentally forgot to shield $150,000 worth of property from probate? She was an attorney, and still missed a detail in a field that was unfamiliar to her.

Also, it is important to recognize that when you are incapacitated or have passed away, you don't get a "do-over." You can't monitor the process after the fact, which is why you have to carefully think through the rules you leave behind.

Finally, appreciate the high stakes. A bad strategy can burden your family and needlessly strip thousands of dollars of value from your estate.

It's not just the fees, taxes, creditor issues... it's that your loved ones will have to clean up the mess.

You should choose wisely with whom you work.

Not every attorney can generate estate plans or work with elders. Complex bodies of law are involved, and you need a specialist.

The Law Offices of Douglas E. Koenig is your trusted Elder Law and Estate Planning attorney. We recognize the importance of your situation. We listen to you. We learn the family dynamics that affect each and every one of your decisions.

In addition, the staff and attorneys at the law offices are compassionate and passionate about elder law. We try to care for our clients as if they were our family. After all, a family member is usually why we got into this field in the first place.

We seek to help families plan for your life transitions. We do this through comprehensive planning and compassionate understanding. We provide the right documents, for the right reasons, at the right time.

Take action now.

I want to thank you for spending time with me. Hopefully, you're now (at least slightly!) less confused by the why's and wherefores of estate planning and also more motivated to get to work on this critical "Quadrant 2" activity.

Your loved ones are counting on you.

Law Offices of Douglas E. Koenig, PLLC
2530 Meridian Parkway, Suite 300, Durham, NC 27713

Normally, I charge prospective clients $1,000 or more for a several hour, thorough discussion about their estate planning goals, but I'd like to offer you a one-hour consultation as a FREE gift. Consider it a "thank you" from me to you for taking the time to read this book and consider its ideas.

Please call my offices at The Law Offices of Douglas E. Koenig, PLLC to schedule this consultation now to obtain the peace of mind and clarity that you deserve!

Call us at
919-724-4778

or reach us at

http://www.dougkoeniglaw.com/EPConsult

About The Author

Attorney Douglas E. Koenig

- Estate Planning
- Medicaid Planning
- Incapacity Planning
- Special Needs Trusts
- Veteran's Benefits (A&A and SCD)

I'm a Navy brat, said in the kindest of terms! As a child in a military family, I understand the unique challenges of military life from that perspective. Yes, moving all over the Gulf Coast, making new friends, and having dad deployed for long periods ... it is what we all went through together. And, as a result,

I appreciate the sacrifice of those who have chosen to serve in the armed forces.

Most recently, I'm a graduate of the Michigan State University College of Law where I was involved in the business law and alternative dispute resolution programs. The College of Law is an established and accomplished institution in many areas and is a top 100 law school at a Big Ten University.

I completed undergraduate work at Dartmouth College and hold a degree in Materials Engineering from Thayer School of Engineering. My history and prior engineering and business experience contribute a strong foundation to my Juris Doctor, and my service to you!

In 2010, I established a compassionate Elder Law practice, which is focused on four main areas, including Veteran's benefits, Medicaid planning and crisis response, Special Needs Trusts, and Estate Planning and the related wills, trusts, and powers of attorney.

Not everyone can afford legal representation, so when appropriate, I offer time and expertise to various programs, including LEAP (via the NC Bar Association), Legal Aid of North Carolina, the UNC Pro Bono Cancer Clinic, and other organizations.

My other service time includes the Durham Downtown Rotary Club and the Gideons.

When we meet, be sure to ask about my work with Digital Equipment Corporation and Ford Motor Company in Michigan prior to locating in North Carolina. I have found connections with my clients through shared work experiences all over the world!

Church matters are important too and so I spend time participating in and leading bible study groups (in case you are invited, Bible Study Fellowship is a wonderful organization!).

I also enjoy sailing, photography, traveling, and, of course, friends and family! This year, my wife and I will have been married for 39 years, and we have three grown children and two grandchildren.

Douglas E. Koenig, Esq.

Law Offices of Douglas E. Koenig, PLLC
2530 Meridian Parkway, Suite 300, Durham, NC 27713

Take Action Today!

Take action today toward CLARITY ABOUT YOUR FUTURE!

Douglas E. Koenig, Esq.

NOTES:

Douglas E. Koenig, Esq.